BOOK ANALYSIS

Written by Caroline Sénécal
Translated by Rose Brichard

AF131382

The Aeneid

BY VIRGIL

VIRGIL

ROMAN POET

- **Born in the village of Andes in roughly 70 BC**
- **Died in Brundisium in 19 BC**
- **Notable works:**
  - *The Eclogues* (42-39 BC), collection of poems known as eclogues or bucolics
  - *The Georgics* (39-29 BC), poem
  - *The Aeneid* (29 BC), epic poem

Nowadays, there are few surviving sources to give us insight into Virgil's life. The poet is thought to have been born around the 15th of October in 70 BC. All that is known for certain about Virgil is the date of his death - the 21st of September 19 BC - twelve years into the Augustan period of Roman history. It is generally agreed that Virgil began writing *The Aeneid* around 29 BC, and that the author worked on it continually until his death. *The Aeneid* is often considered as one of the greatest works to emerge from Roman antiquity as it has inspired generations of authors ever since.

THE AENEID

FROM THE TROJAN WAR TO THE BIRTH OF ROME

- **Genre**: poetry (epic)
- **Reference edition:** Virgil (29 BC) *The Aeneid*. [online]. Trans. Mackail, J. W., 2007. Project Guthenberg. [Accessed 20th July 2016]. Available from: <http://www.gutenberg.org/files/22456/22456-h/22456-h.htm#BOOK_SECOND>
- **First edition:** 29 BC
- **Themes**: history, ancient Rome, mythology, the Trojan War

Although Emperor Augustus originally commissioned Virgil to write *The Aeneid*, the epic poem is far from a mere tool of the State. It constitutes something much more than a moral, social and political project or a piece of imperial propaganda. In fact, Virgil refused to focus his work on recent history, instead turning towards the ancient founding myth of Aeneas, the mythical founder of Rome, and the glorious history of Roman civilisation and the Trojan War. Through his work, Virgil seeks to unify all Italic peoples around shared Roman values. *The Aeneid* follows the story of its hero Aeneas through various adventures and episodes as he establishes himself in Italy and lays the foundation for the Roman power and civilisation which will emerge in the years to come.

The Aeneid is a rich and complex literary work, and also features a tragic love story between two now legendary figures: Aeneas and Dido.

SUMMARY

The Aeneid is a work in twelve volumes which alternate between stories of great adventure and long passages where the plot itself does not advance.

The poem can be roughly divided into two halves:

* The first six books tell the story of Aeneas, a Trojan born to a mortal father named Anchises and the goddess Venus. In these books, Aeneas and his companions wander in search of a land spoken of in a prophecy from the oracle. This epic journey is reminiscent of Ulysses' voyage after the Trojan War. Furthermore, some elements of Virgil's story explicitly draw on *The Odyssey* by Homer (Greek epic poet, 8th century BC) - particularly with regards to the cyclops.
* Books VI-XII on the other hand can be linked to *The Iliad*, and tell the story of the political intrigues and conflicts related to the Trojan War and how its survivors constructed a new society in Italy.

BOOK I - SETTING THE SCENE

Seven years after the Trojan War, Aeneas is forced to take shelter in Carthage amid a terrible storm. Jupiter predicts that the Trojans will establish themselves in Italy and found Rome. This book also tells the story of the first encounter between Aeneas and Dido, the queen of Carthage. In the evening, the Trojans are invited to dine. During the banquet, the queen asks Aeneas to recount the story of his voyage across the Mediterranean.

BOOKS II AND III - THE SIEGE OF TROY AND THE LONG JOURNEY: TALES WITHIN A TALE

These two books tell the epic tale of the hero and his adventures since the fall of his hometown - Troy - until the day he arrives in Carthage.

Aeneas opens his story with the tale of the Trojan Horse (p. 25-26) and the city being ransacked during the night (p. 27-32). The Greeks lay siege upon the sleeping city with the help of Ulysses' trickery. Hector, the fallen Trojan prince, appears to Aeneas in a dream and tells him that Troy has fallen and implores him to take the Penates (Roman household deities) and the gods to safety outside of the city. When he awakes, he first tries to fight against the enemy, but his mother Venus comes to him and tells him that his destiny awaits him outside Troy. He flees the city with his father, his son, and other Trojan survivors of the massacre.

During his voyage, Aeneas has to deal with much adversity. Virgil highlights several of his adventures, such as his landing in Buthrotum. Book III primarily focuses on various prophecies made about Aeneas and his destiny:

- On the island of Delos, Apollo speaks to Aeneas and tells him that he should go to found a new city on the land of his Trojan ancestors;
- The Penates tell Aeneas that he must go to Latium, the land where the founding father of Troy had his origins;

- One of the Harpies (female monsters with wings and claws) named Celaeno predicts that Aeneas will only found his city after great suffering and famine;
- Helenus, King of Epirus, advises Aeneas to go to the Sibyl and tells him that he will know this is the land he is searching for when he sees a white sow suckling thirty piglets.

BOOK IV - AENEAS AND DIDO: A LOVE STORY

Dido falls in love with Aeneas. During a storm, Aeneas and Dido take refuge in a cave and consummate their love for one another (p. 75). However, Mercury soon arrives to remind Aeneas of his quest, and he leaves Dido behind (p. 79).

The final 300 lines of book IV are dedicated to Dido, distraught and heartbroken. She curses Aeneas for abandoning her and kills herself.

BOOK V - PASSING THROUGH SICILY AND PLAYING WITH DEATH

After departing from Carthage, Aeneas and his crew are forced to stop on Sicily where they are taken in by King Acestes, a fellow Trojan. This is where Aeneas had buried his father one year previously; it is the first anniversary of his death. Aeneas organises games in honour of his late father.

Aeneas decides to leave the weakest of his travelling Trojans behind in Sicily after Juno convinces the women, who are weary of travelling, to set fire to the ships. Just as Neptune wished, a man loses his life during the crossing towards

Latium - Palinurus the captain. Anchises' spirit appears to his son and tells him to visit him in the underworld when he arrives in Italy.

BOOK VI - DESCENT INTO THE UNDERWORLD

Aeneas consults the Sibyl when he arrives in Cumae. The priestess predicts that the Trojans have hardship and war ahead of them. Aeneas asks her to take him to the underworld to see his father. There, he finds Anchises, who tells his son what will happen to his future descendants and how the Roman world will develop right up until the time of Augustus. Aeneas comes back to the surface of the earth and heads towards Latium.

BOOK VII - THE ARRIVAL IN LATIUM

Aeneas arrives in Latium and King Latinus is expecting him. He himself has spoken with oracles who have warned him that his daughter Lavinia should not marry Turnus, the Rutulian king (an ancient people from south of Latium). She is instead destined to marry a foreigner, and their marriage is to produce great figures who are born to rule. Juno sends Alecto, one of her Furies (Roman goddesses of vengeance) to wreak havoc between Latinus' and Turnus' people; violent conflict is inevitable.

BOOK VIII - TOWARDS WAR

Tiberius, god of the Tiber river, appears to Aeneas in a dream and reassures him of his destiny, urging him to make an alliance with Evander of Arcadia. When he awakes, Aeneas sees the prophesied sow and sacrifices it to Juno. On the way, he comes across Evander who is in the middle of a religious ceremony and asks Aeneas to join him. Aeneas then goes to Arcadia with the king where he shows him this city and his palace.

Aeneas and Evander form an alliance with the Tuscans (ancient Italic people), and together plan to lead a revolt against the tyrant Mezentius who is currently being harboured by Turnus. Evander puts some of his troops at Aeneas' disposition, led by his son Pallas. Venus appears to Aeneas and gives him the arms he needs to win the battle.

BOOK IX - THE BATTLES

Far from the camp, Aeneas seeks out new alliances. Turnus leads his army towards the enemy camp where they try to set fire to the Trojan ships.

Following on from this, several battles take place: Nisus and Euryalus against the Rutulis, and Ascanius against Numanus. Turnus penetrates the city and kills several men. He then finds himself trapped in the enemy camp and jumps into the river to escape.

BOOKS X AND XI - THE LIBERATION OF THE CAMP, THE DEATH OF PALLAS AND MEZENTIUS AND THE BURIAL OF THE DEAD

The Trojans are still under siege. A nymph warns Aeneas of

the situation and he returns to the camp. Mezentius and Pallas are killed, but the Trojans emerge victorious from the battle.

In Book XI, both sides agree on a truce to allow them to bury their dead. Aeneas ensures Pallas has a hero's funeral. He proposes that he and Turnus engage in a duel, but Turnus rejects the idea and the hostilities quickly recommence. The heroic Camilla, the Volscian queen, appears in the middle of a cavalry battle and is killed by Arruns, the Tuscan leader. The Latin army is defeated.

BOOK XII - TURNUS' DEATH AND AENEAS' VICTORY

Turnus prepares for his battle with Aeneas and his troops after King Latinus tries to convince him to end the war and give up on his daughter Lavinia.

Juno sends Juturna, Turnus' sister, disguised as one of the troops, to encourage them to defend Turnus against Aeneas. The battle erupts and Aeneas is wounded, but is healed by his mother. He re-enters the battle with a successful counterattack. Various developments in the battle occur and new twists in the tale mean it remains unresolved. Jupiter calls Juturna back. Aeneas and Turnus enter into a duel and Aeneas defeats Turnus, killing him even though he begs for mercy.

CHARACTER STUDY

AENEUS

Aeneus is the hero and protagonist of Virgil's epic poem. He is the consummate epic hero - he is of noble blood and the son of Anchises, a mortal, and the goddess Venus, making him a demigod. He is a brave and valiant warrior, fighting with pride throughout his amazing adventures. His fellow Trojans describe him as such: "foremost of men in righteousness, incomparable in goodness as in warlike arms;" (Book I, p. 17). Furthermore, he is compared to other mythological heroes and even to gods on several occasions throughout the text. As a leader, he is entirely dedicated to his duty and places his own interests below those of the group; it is for this reason that he sacrifices his love for Dido to continue his mission. He is also a hero who receives divine support, with gods predicting the great destiny which awaits him.

However, Virgil's protagonist is more than a superhuman hero; he is a complex figure with a truly human dimension. He has serious doubts, laments his lot in life, shows signs of remorse with regards to his love for Dido (Book IV, p. 83) and even finds the thought of war revolting (Book XI, p. 121/122). His relationship with Dido represents the human dimension of the character; amid his passion, Aeneas forgets his mission and succumbs to his emotions towards Dido, temporarily reducing his heroic status.

Aeneas is the true incarnation of ancient Roman values: *fides* (fidelity, respect for orders, loyalty), *pietas* (faith, devotion, patriotism, duty), *majestas* (a feeling of natural superiority and of belonging to the chosen people), *virtus* (courage, political activity), and *gravitas* (respect for tradition, dignity, authority). His religious devotion and respect for Roman customs can also be viewed in this light; after all, he is called "Pious Aeneas". Virgil keeps his hero's virtue utterly intact; with little said on the matter, the reader must deduce for themselves that a sexual act has taken place between Aeneas and Dido in the cave. Furthermore, Virgil does not criticise Aeneas for leaving Dido. Since remarrying was considered total debauchery by the Romans, it was clear that to adhere to the value system of the time, the widow Dido's affections towards Aeneas could only lead to disappointment. Virgil instead highlights Aeneas' spirituality and character as a hero who respects Roman values and is ready to cast aside his love for his grand mission.

Aeneas is the founding father of a civilisation, the champion of Roman values and a true hero.

DIDO

Dido's character departs from the norms of the normal female role in Roman literature and culture. Virgil's female lead is not a classic Roman maternal figure who kills herself for the sake of honour; instead, this queen is a truly tragic character. Dido represents the humiliation of passion, committing suicide after being abandoned. Throughout Book IV, Dido and Aeneas' characters develop as truly contrasting roles: she represents romantic love, while he embodies spiritual love. It should be noted that Virgil also uses imagery to construct this opposition, speaking of light and dark, order and disorder, etc.

The figure of Dido has gone down in history and been brought back to life by many artists and writers, such as Purcell, who wrote an opera named Dido and Aeneas (1689). She now has truly mythical status in the cultural sphere.

TURNUS

Turnus is Aeneas' enemy, but an epic hero in his own right. He is a gallant warrior, and is compared to the god Mars in Book III. Parts of the text are devoted to his own adventures. Like Aeneas, he too conforms to the image of the ideal Roman hero and Roman customs and values, as shown by the ritual at the declaration of war in Book IX. As such, he is a truly worthy adversary for Aeneas. The similarities between Aeneas and Turnus are even shown in their weapons - both Turnus' sword and Aeneas' shield were made by Vulcan.

In contrast to this, Turnus is inferior to Aeneas when it comes to his humanity and compassion - perhaps even his opposite. When he kills Pallas, he shows the cruel side of his nature, in contrast to Aeneas who only kills young Lausus with great reluctance (Book X, p. 242). Turnus is impulsive and often succumbs to fits of rage and anger. In this light, the two heroes are constructed in total contrast to one another, with Virgil painting Aeneas as serene and deliberative and Turnus as savage and impulsive. It should be noted that Turnus is also abandoned by the gods.

THE GODS

The gods play a crucial role in Virgil's work, presiding over the destiny of all the characters. Human fate is subject to their will, alliances and disagreements. While Juno contributed to the fall of Troy and tried to stop Aeneas from fulfilling his destiny, this is due to a dispute between her and Venus (the "apple of discord" myth), the hero's mother. For this reason, the goddess does everything in her power to thwart Aeneas on his mission, blocking his path with terrible storms and sending other gods to hold him back from founding Rome. Divine intervention in human actions is a classic trope of epic poetry, but is also illustrative of the religious beliefs of Virgil's time.

Throughout the entire poem, oracles also have particular importance, providing prophecies and other divine messages which shape the plot development. For example, Anchises refuses to leave until he sees a sign from the gods; an oracle tells Latinus that his daughter must marry someone foreign, and Aeneas views the appearance of new weapons as a gift from his mother. Other more implicit phenomena also foreshadow Aeneas' glorious destiny. For example, Venus stops Aeneas from killing Helen of Troy (Book II, p. 42), and Hector, Creusa and Anchises visit Aeneas in his sleep. It is also worth noting that certain scenes are actually narrated by the gods themselves, further cementing the idea that humans are subject to their will and plans.

ANALYSIS

THE EPIC AS A GENRE

The epic is the most prestigious literary genre in the Western classical tradition. Epics are long narrative poems which mix history and mythology. They also celebrate the exploits and adventures of heroes who must overcome great difficulties and hardship to reach their goal. This genre has several characteristics, all of which can be found in *The Aeneid*:

- As Aristotle notes in his *Poetics*, epics are grand and noble in their characters, plotlines and their style. In terms of characters, Aeneas fits the bill as a demigod who belongs to a long line of heroes. In its plotline, the heroes in *The Aeneid* achieve unthinkable feats on the road to their grand destinies. With regards to style, Virgil deliberately writes in a very grandiose manner with a grave and solemn tone;
- Epics also have a supernatural dimension which often takes the form of divine intervention, as is the case in *The Aeneid*;
- There is a strong political presence in the work. The epic usually follows a hero who is guided by duty, often that of founding a new civilisation. In *The Aeneid*, Aeneas' duty is to found Rome;
- The rhetoric used in the epic is highly codified. Since epics are based in the oral tradition, most authors of these texts use expressive language and strong imagery in their writing. Virgil does exactly that, using many literary devices to build the mood such as lists and repetition. For

example, in Book V the author describes the games on Sicily in great detail; in Book VII he discusses all of the troops in the battle, and in Books IX and X, he outlines each and every aspect of the war. Virgil is keen to bolster his hero and his achievements and shows the superiority of his characters through the use of superlatives and hyperbole, or with magnificent similes and imagery. He often compares his heroes to gods, animals or even forces of nature. For example, Aeneas is likened to Apollo when he goes hunting (Book IV, p. 181), and Turnus compared to a wolf (Book IX, p. 194).

THE PLACE OF THE LOVE STORY IN THE EPIC

Book IV momentarily halts the epic quest and allows the story to veer off towards love and romanticism. Aeneas stops in Carthage and meets Dido in a fateful encounter. It is a true high point of the work, with Virgil dramatically presenting the tension and clash between duty and love, the individual and the group and gods and human responsibility. This book also inserts an element of tragedy into the overall glorious tale.

In Book IV, Virgil follows the classic codes of tragedy:

- The way the lovers' feelings for each other develop is in line with storylines of literature's greatest tragedies. Firstly, passion erupts within Dido, then she admits this to Anna and recognises the love she feels; next, a honeymoon period occurs where the characters feel free from the calls of duty; this is followed by a moment of crisis full of suffering and self-sabotage; next, a dramatic twist (Aeneas leaves and abandons his love); lastly, the queen kills herself;

- *The Aeneid* also conforms to the classical unities law, i.e. unity of time, place and action. Virgil adapts time to follow the action; while Aeneas' voyages take years, he only spends three months in Carthage and as soon as he and Dido admit their love for one another, the pace of the action quickly increases. Most of the action takes place in the palace and focuses almost entirely on the love story between the two heroes;

- Passion is linked to suffering. Virgil's poetic language serves to highlight the dangerous side of passion. This is displayed most notably in his word choice, speaking of physical and emotional pain, madness, violence and rage. Dido is often aligned with other mythical figures which symbolises the rupture with the civilised world through the fervour of her passion for Aeneas. Virgil also uses imagery of fire and flames to portray Dido's desire. Dialogues between other characters develop an element of catharsis in the work and guide the reader towards a view that passion is a destructive force. Just as is the case with classical tragedies, Book IV's storyline equally serves to punish forbidden love in presenting a sensible hero who condemns Dido's irrational behaviour and privileges his duty and mission. Through this, Virgil illustrates a certain vision of morality and adds a cautionary air to the tale;

- There is a clash between love and duty. This tension appears frequently in the great tragedies. When Aeneas chooses his mission over romantic love, he affirms that moral and social duty is superior to passion. He puts an end to the disorder which comes from his romance and allows his followers to return to their quest, meaning the epic can continue. Dido is the victim in Virgil's narrative and serves to glorify Rome;

- The outcome is tragic, with Dido committing suicide. The hero's tragic demise is often linked to transgression; when Dido imagines a life with Aeneas, she is transgressing a crucial social code that widows must not remarry. Thus, her death can also be viewed through a lens of guilt with regards to social norms and institutions. In her death she frees herself from this culpability.

A RITE OF PASSAGE

Aeneas' voyage is not only a physical one but also an emotional journey. Through this, Virgil draws a subtle parallel between the quest for new lands and the inner quest for the true self. Furthermore, the aim of finding new land is there to allow for the birth of a new people, thus reinforcing the notion of identity and selfhood in the text. Aeneas' character evolves throughout the text and a clear contrast can be seen between his nature at the start and the end of the poem. He is initially naive - as shown in the incident with the Trojan Horse where he is ready to kill Helen of Troy.

During his voyage, he begs for help from the gods and bemoans his lot in life (Book I, p. 3); here, he becomes a hero in the making. In the middle of the storm, he evokes the legendary Trojan warriors, and in many ways this foreshadows his own destiny. He affirms his status as a true hero in the course of the action through his various adventures. He develops confidence in himself and devotion to his mission. In Book X, he is sure that he will win his battle with Turnus.

The poem therefore takes on an educational character, where Aeneas' journey becomes a rite of passage to maturity and enlightenment. Aeneas' quest is littered with moral and physical obstacles and trials; from each of these, he learns a lesson, as does the reader. One of his first tests is the death of his father Anchises. This elevates Aeneas to the head of his familial line and gives him a true grounding as a future patriarch. The death of Aeneas' wet nurse on arrival in Italy is also a symbolic event as he matures. At every step of his journey, Aeneas loses a comrade or someone close to him (Creusa, Anchises, Dido). This crystallises the notion that the steps towards adulthood are at the cost of loss and pain. The ultimate example of this is in Carthage where he avoids the temptation to abandon his quest and stay with Dido.

Aeneas evolves as a warrior, as a lover, and at a spiritual level:

- He has little involvement in the combat during the Trojan War, but in the second part of the poem, he accomplishes a number of feats on the battlefield. He becomes a brave and valiant warrior, shown ultimately by his victory over Turnus;
- While Aeneas is the embodiment of the masculine Roman ideal and has an acute awareness of his duties towards the gods, the poem also places emphasis on his spiritual education and development. This is shown through his

interaction with oracles, his descent into the underworld and the games in honour of Anchises, for example.

Aeneas succeeded in resisting the call of passion, reflecting on his situation and turning towards love without the element of excess.

FURTHER REFLECTION

SOME QUESTIONS TO THINK ABOUT...

- How does the tragic love in Book IV of *The Aeneid* contrast with the erotic love in Roman erotic elegies? Discuss in relation to the *Georgics* and the *Eclogues*.
- Dido's character is the source of a truly legendary character in literature: the woman who is madly in love and kills herself after being abandoned by her lover. Can you draw any parallels between Dido and other figures of tragedy such as Racine's Phèdre or Andromaque?
- What role do the gods play in *The Aeneid*?
- Virgil takes inspiration from Homer not only with regards to the structure of his poems, but also certain lines and literary techniques, such as the story within a story (mise-en-abyme). Just like Homer, he writes about mythological characters and generations of illustrious families. Find the Homeric intertext in Virgil's work. What role does it play in *The Aeneid*?
- Aeneas' descent into the underworld (Book VI) plays on popular beliefs, myths and philosophy regarding the afterlife; can you find evidence of this?
- What are the elements linking to the concept of a rite of passage in the epic poem?
- Describe Virgil's writing style.

We want to hear from you!
Leave a comment on your online library
and share your favourite books on social media!

FURTHER READING

REFERENCE EDITION

- Virgil (29 BC) *The Aeneid*. [online]. Trans. Mackail, J. W., 2007. Project Guthenberg. [Accessed 20th July 2016]. Available from: <http://www.gutenberg.org/files/22456/22456-h/22456-h.htm#BOOK_SECOND>

REFERENCE STUDIES

- Constans, L.-A. (1938) L'Énéide *de Virgile. Étude et analyse*. Paris: Librairie Mellottée.
- Dion, J. (1993) *Les Passions dans l'oeuvre de Virgile. Poétique et philosophie*. Nancy: Presses Universitaires de Nancy.
- Grimal, P. (1963) *L'Amour à Rome*. Paris: Librairie Hachette.

©BrightSummaries.com, 2016. All rights reserved.

www.brightsummaries.com

Ebook EAN: 9782806280350

Paperback EAN: 9782806283030

Legal Deposit: D/2016/12603/322

Cover: © Primento

Digital conception by Primento, the digital partner of publishers.